the samurai

by
Linda M. Crate

illustrations by
Ann Marie Sekeres

YELLOW ARROW
PUBLISHING
Baltimore, Maryland, USA

the samurai
Copyright © 2020 by Yellow Arrow Publishing
All rights reserved.

Library of Congress Control Number: 2020945687
ISBN (paperback): 978-1-7350230-2-1

Illustrations by Ann Marie Sekeres (annmarieprojects.com). Interior design by Yellow Arrow Publishing (yellowarrowpublishing.com).

Contents

acknowledgments	1
1. lost in translation	5
2. my past self & i	7
3. there'll always be dirt	9
4. i will never give this up	11
5. the old souls speak	13
6. finding balance	15
7. she remembered my courage	17
8. she has her sword	19
9. the samurai . . .	21
10. every monster will fall	23
11. birds of a feather	27
12. she softly whispered	29
13. the kindest moonlight	31
14. a grave that was not mine	33
15. the shadows are behind me	35
16. i won't bow nor apologize	37
17. my stubborn heart	39
18. a warrior never surrenders	41
19. my dreams are my sword	43

20. i won't stop fighting	45
21. there is no surrender	47
about the author	49

acknowledgments

Chantarelle's Notebook (online), February 2020
"my past self & i"

THE SAMURAI

1. lost in translation

the samurai
i once was
taught me the
courage
i have now,
and all that is to come

she was valiant
and she was magnificent

her face was schooled,
betraying none of her emotions;
my face betrays all of mine

perhaps some things
were lost in translation.

2. my past self & i

my fear of heights,
and climbing on roofs
specifically
now makes sense after the dream;

she was fighting on a roof
when she died
and she fell and i fell until she could not wake—

now i am anew
with flesh and a body
that is mine but wasn't then,

maybe that's why these bones
feel out of place sometimes;

i recall who i was and who i am is not always
the same as recollections buried
in my subconscious,
little seeds of doubt and curiosity singing together
a medley of magic only my soul can decipher.

3. there'll always be dirt

i know now
why i am afraid of heights
why i never have any inclination
to climb a rooftop;
i wonder was she someone
loved and respected,
admired and adored?
or was she sometimes like the monsters
i so detest;
i have so much love in me
that i'd like to say no,
but i have so much rage
that i can blaze like an inferno in the dead
of night and light the world—
perhaps no matter how good we are,
we'll always be monsters;
we try to wash off the dirt but there
will always be soil even after we've been buried.

4. i will never give this up

when i first recalled her, i remembered who i truly was; a fierce, courageous fighter—i was done trying to water myself down for the approval of others, reclaimed my voice and my mysticism (i know i am too much for some and too little for others but i am perfectly me)—i won't be caged in the expectations of others because i know who i am, and i don't need anyone to define me other than myself; i love myself and that's what truly matters because i am the one i will be spending my life with—i won't drown waiting for the validation of others because in the end what others think of me doesn't matter, they don't have my heart or my depth; as i gaze back, i realize i've always fought for what i believe in—
                    i will always fight for what i believe in because i refuse to live without dreams or hope, i will always break through the chaos with my love and my light and i will fight for myself and those that have been rendered voiceless by the world because we all deserve to be who we truly are; i will never give this up—it has been sewn into my being for a reason.

5. the old souls speak

she was wearing a red kimono when she passed, maybe that's why red is my favorite color; the hue of love, passion, the one that urges us to stop, and the one we see when we're angry; the color of setting suns and my birthstone in this life—

the threads we weave follow us from lifetime to lifetime, perhaps when we get that feeling of déjà vu it's our past selves warning us of a hidden danger in a situation we didn't consider; perhaps it is something we've lived before, tethered to the past; we have a future in new bones but the old incantations are telling us secrets if only we'd listen to their wisdom, but so many people ignore their inner voices as they seem to follow after a crowd that doesn't even recall their true name; but i know who i am and strive to be the best me i can be—in the end we can only be the people we give ourselves room to become and i am limitless, going to be the best being i can be; because as flawed and imperfect as i am, i am beautiful, i am enchanted, i am powerful; a warrior of love and light.

6. finding balance

once
an old classmate
told of a past life
she had,
and i was skeptical
until i saw the samurai in my mind's eye—
beautiful and powerful
she stood on that precipice
full of discipline and fury,
unwavering in her aim;
her battle she lost
when her feet
became dislodged and she fell
perhaps that is why i am always uneasy
when unbalanced
in one way or another,
and i thank her for this wisdom;
it has saved me from falling
once or twice into situations that would've
been tricky to get out of.

7. she remembered my courage

life has many lessons
i think it is
important to know
the past

because when i saw
who i once was,
my valor and nerve
returned to me
as if it had never disappeared;

i let go of that scared
little rabbit
embraced the golden crimson wings
of the immortal phoenix

burned away every bridge of the past
that didn't serve me—

she taught me that my fear
wasn't just something random and irrational,
but something that didn't work
in my favor
before;

now i'm always looking for balanced traction
so i don't trip into death before my time.

8. she has her sword

one thing she had
that i do not
is a sword

every time i see one
i want to hold it,

and i think that is her
influence;
she knows the ways
of combat

she won't let me forget
who i am—
i am grateful that whatever
buried her from me finally unearthed her in my mind
so i could know that i am more, much more, than i
ever believed i was.

9. the samurai . . .

. . . murmured
to me of my métier,
stubbornly reminded me
never to give up;
she helped me
leech out
fear and insecurities,
and whilst both still remain,
she helped me regain my ferocity
not just my
vulnerability.

. . . woke me up when i was confused
in a dark nightmare,
and i will forever be grateful
for the starlight she put back in my eyes
when i thought all was gone;
i was just shedding unnecessary things
so i could become me.

10. every monster will fall

when i forgot who i was
she didn't,
she brought back the
laughter in my life

when i thought his gaze
upon my flesh
was always going to be cold,

she broke up the winter
left behind in my heart

reminded me
that i was summer's stubborn daughter,
and that i couldn't let the light in me
die before my time;

so i shook off the shackles of the past

as she reminded me
to learn from,
not leave my past behind

and now i stand knowing
that i am a fighter and a survivor,
victim no longer because i refuse to
yield myself before my nightmares.

every monster will fall before my sword.

11. birds of a feather

silent and robust
two things
we have in common

i'm a woman
of a few words
but a million emotions;
i think she was better
at hiding her expressions
because even if my words
are scant my face
tells all—

i've not mastered
every art
she has
and vice versa;

we are tethered together
for a reason,
and i trust her;
she woke me when i dragged myself in pain stuck
in the dredges of a tea that was never mine to drink,
trapped with the monster i could not seem to slay.

12. she softly whispered

her hair was long, too
but black as
the wings of crows and ravens—

mine is woven with every hue of autumn:
red, brown, gold;
and whilst it is pretty i always wished
for hair like hers

i prefer darker hair and eyes
in my partners, too—

i sense she was caught in the tongue of
an unrequited love,
and i have known that misery, too

yet despite all the pain there is a sweetness
to life and i think she knew that—

it's why she softly whispered
her name and her life so i always remember
that i am bold, i am everlasting, i am daring;
that i am more than tears
and the mistake of loving a man who couldn't love me.

13. the kindest moonlight

we both know the misery of unrequited love; perhaps it was the reason she fell—perhaps a broken heart was the reason she slipped from the ridge that day despite giving it her all. sometimes the villains win and the heroes fall, which makes me more determined to win this time because there are too many nightmares and too much chaos in this world—we need places of tranquility and places of hope, so i am letting my light shine so that everyone can know we need not dwell in the darkness always; sometimes night is kind and sometimes she is cruel and life is often bittersweet—but i choose to focus on the kindest moonlight, the laughing waters which wash away all my troubles and sorrows for a while, all the trees that hug me back with wisdom when i hug their bodies, every lyric of an honest wind singing to me myths and truths of old and new, every majestic crow, every color of the rainbow dancing in the sky, and sunshine which is actually warm; i know there will always be bad things but there is goodness in this world worth fighting for and i will stand my ground.

14. a grave that was not mine

her actions spoke louder than her words, she opened doors in me that i didn't know existed; she pushed me to the warmth of my friends and family when i wanted nothing more than to wallow in the pain and let it rip me apart in all of its aching—i think she knew that i needed someone to thrust me forward because i didn't know how to move except to drag myself with the monsters of the past as my baggage, and she sent them packing with one swift slash of her sword. and the look she gave me reminded me that in the Chinese zodiac i am the tiger—ferocious and regal and roaring—so i knew my claws and slashed through the throat of every painful memory weighing me down and began to live again, letting myself to be bathed in the warmth of laughter and love and fond remembrances; showered myself with the petals of flowers and the waters of oceans and creeks and the audience of trees and ferns and spells; i felt my power and snatched back my spells and my divinity—the girl that lay murdered in that coffin broke through the wood and nails and soil as if they never existed.
i departed a grave that was not mine.

15. the shadows are behind me

she was the hand reaching for mine from behind the glass of the mirror, she was the one that pulled me into the future, urging me to leave the past behind—she knew i was sturdier than the worn down island of misery i had become, she knew i had a purpose in this world; to be a victor not victim—i was never born to be anyone's conquest, i am full of enchantment and depths, and if someone can't appreciate me for who i am then they don't deserve my time nor my love but i will never regret being me. i won't let anyone change me. my spirit will always pursue the light and the visions that lead me to the fires that make me happiest because life is too short to stand in the shadows, so i will face heaven and let him burn away the shadows behind me.

16. i won't bow nor apologize

i will bow before no one in shame
because i know despite all my mistakes and failures
i have found wisdom and forté,

the light in my eyes shines brighter than the
stars shimmering in the sky,
rivaling even the light of my mother, the moon,
because i am too stubborn to give up—

we refuse to give up,
and perhaps my intensity is something that drives a wedge
between me and those not meant to be in my life;

i will not apologize for my depths or my heights
or anything between because i am limitless and i refuse to be
anyone less than me because anything else is a lie and i have
    always
shunned liars.

17. my stubborn heart

we are spirited
full of fire, full of fury, full of ferocity;
there is an intensity that ties us together
despite all the time between us—

when i thought all was gone
she revealed the puzzle of me
that now makes better sense;

i am not afraid of my power now
because i know that i have and will always be
tougher than i realize because i have a stubborn heart
refusing to give in and cave to the nightmares

trying to drag me away from my reveries
and tear from me who i truly am to convince me that
somehow i am lesser than who i am—
because of her, i know no matter what, i am immortal of the
    flame.

18. a warrior never surrenders

he was a red herring,
the false ending
i thought
was mine;
a love unrequited.
i ended up wounding myself
because i cared too much for someone
who cared too little—
his apology wasn't an apology,
just words thrown together
purposefully to wound me;
and i thought i was going to close myself up
from the world, completely
shrivel up and die, lonely and cold—
but i rose anew because
she helped wake me from a slumber
i mistook for death—
i was reassured by the flowers
that i would bloom again,
and i took up her sword as mine
because a fighter never succumbs to oblivion.

19. my dreams are my sword

she tapped me on my shoulder, grabbed my hand, and pushed me into the future; i must leave behind all my self-doubt and criticisms—recognize that i am not the beast nor the blame of the terrible things he did to me, rise on amber and ruby wings, immortal and tireless—knowing that no matter what, i will not submit to death (that is too insulting for the life i have yet to live). some women walk in the shadows, but i am meant to blaze with eternal light and dance with the flowers and the trees and the creeks—even at night the kindest moonlight keeps me company; i hold my dreams like she held her katana and i will slice through as many people as need be should they stand in the way of my reveries—because in this world of nightmares, i am not willing to let the darkness swallow me anymore.

20. i won't stop fighting

i trust her
because she woke me up,
shook my self-wallowing—
she stood so tall in her red kimono
sprinkled with flecks of golden stars,
the phoenix first before i was given
these flames;
she could've let me wither and die
become bitter and colder than the one who
left me in the wooden coffin—
yet she refused,
and did not give up on me;
i now have the power
not to give up on myself—
the samurai in me still lives through me and so i make my
dreams, my words, my light a sword against
the darkness of this world;
i won't stop fighting even if i must tread
upon heights and upon precipices.

21. there is no surrender

i woke up
realizing her,
realizing
my magic was mine
as was my voice and my power—
many monsters walk
disguised as humans
with flesh and blood and hearts
but only black holes where their
hearts ought to be,
and anyone who seeks to destroy me
will be slain;

i am more than my
scars—
bringer of love and light,
i will never submit;
stubbornly i hold onto hope and love,
because i know there is goodness in this world worth
fighting for—
there are suns, flowers, moonlight, forests, waters,
reveries, laughter, butterflies, kittens, foxes, puppies, wolves,
music, art, books, life, love, desserts, and well-meaning strangers
who have cheered me on and supported me in dark moments,
including the samurai who took my hand and
    refused to let me go.

Linda M. Crate is a Pennsylvanian born in Pittsburgh but raised in Conneautville. Her work has been published in numerous magazines and anthologies, both online and in print. She is the author of six poetry chapbooks, the latest of which is *More Than Bone Music* (March 2019). She also is the author of the novel *Phoenix Tears* (June 2018) and two micropoetry collections. Recently, she has published two full-length poetry collections, *Vampire Daughter* (February 2020) and *The Sweetest Blood* (February 2020). Linda is also a two-time Pushcart nominee.

Follow her on Facebook, Instagram (@authorlindamcrate), or Twitter (@thysilverdoe).

Thank you for supporting independent publishing.

Yellow Arrow Publishing is a nonprofit supporting writers that identify as women. Visit YellowArrowPublishing.com for information on our publications, workshops, and writing opportunities.

www.ingramcontent.com/pod-product-compliance
Lightning Source LLC
Chambersburg PA
CBHW021133080526
44587CB00012B/1263